COUNTRIES

CHINA

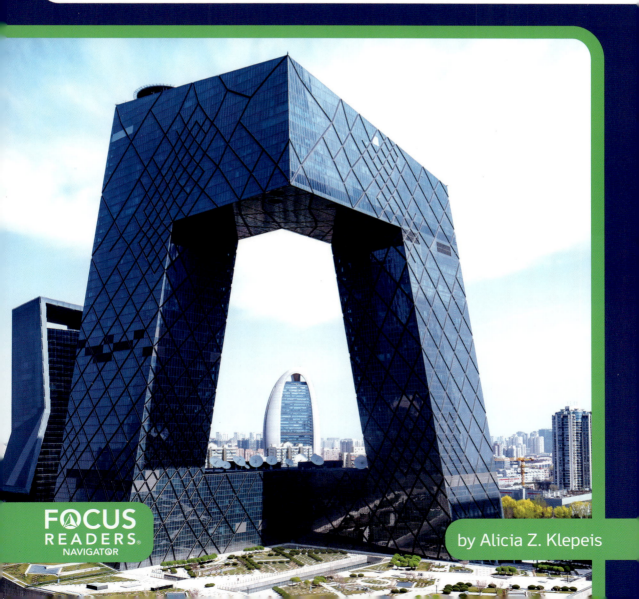

by Alicia Z. Klepeis

FOCUS READERS®
NAVIGATOR

WWW.FOCUSREADERS.COM

Copyright © 2025 by Focus Readers®, Mendota Heights, MN 55120. All rights reserved. No part of this book may be reproduced or utilized in any form or by any means without written permission from the publisher.

Focus Readers is distributed by North Star Editions:
sales@northstareditions.com | 888-417-0195

Produced for Focus Readers by Red Line Editorial.

Content Consultant: Zhao Ma, PhD, Associate Professor of Modern Chinese History, Washington University in St. Louis

Photographs ©: Shutterstock Images, cover, 1, 7, 8–9, 10, 13, 14–15, 20–21, 26–27; iStockphoto, 4–5, 16, 23, 25; Chinatopix/AP Images, 19; Heritage Art/Heritage Images/Hulton Archive/Getty Images, 29

Library of Congress Cataloging-in-Publication Data
Library of Congress Cataloging-in-Publication Data is available on the Library of Congress website.

ISBN
979-8-88998-219-7 (hardcover)
979-8-88998-275-3 (paperback)
979-8-88998-381-1 (ebook pdf)
979-8-88998-331-6 (hosted ebook)

Printed in the United States of America
Mankato, MN
012025

ABOUT THE AUTHOR

Alicia Z. Klepeis began her career at the National Geographic Society. A former middle school teacher, she is the author of numerous children's books, including *Go Wild! Frogs* and *Secrets of the Forest: 15 Bedtime Stories Inspired by Nature*. Alicia loves bringing the world to young readers through her books and school visits.

TABLE OF CONTENTS

CHAPTER 1
Welcome to China 5

CHAPTER 2
History 9

CHAPTER 3
Climate, Plants, and Animals 15

CLIMATE CRISIS IN CHINA
Big Issues 18

CHAPTER 4
Resources, Economy, and Government 21

CHAPTER 5
People and Culture 27

Focus Questions • 30
Glossary • 31
To Learn More • 32
Index • 32

CHAPTER 1

WELCOME TO CHINA

China is a vast country in East Asia. It stretches more than 3,200 miles (5,150 km) both from west to east and from north to south. China borders 14 other countries. Its longest borders are with Russia and Mongolia in the north.

To the east, China touches the Yellow Sea, the East China Sea, and the South

The Great Wall of China stretches for thousands of miles near the country's northern border.

China Sea. Within China are many rivers. The Yangtze and Yellow Rivers are the longest. Both begin on the Tibetan Plateau. This area of high land covers much of western China. From there, rivers flow east to where the land is lower.

Mountains cover about one-third of China. The Himalayas stretch along its southwest border. Mount Everest is part of this range. It is Earth's highest peak.

Eastern China has many lowland areas. People often farm these plains, especially near rivers. Beijing, China's capital, is in eastern China. This huge city has more than 21 million residents. Only one city in China is bigger. Shanghai is home to more than 24 million people. It is in eastern China as well. But other regions also have megacities. Those are cities with more than 10 million people.

MAP OF CHINA

KAZAKHSTAN

RUSSIA

KYRGYZSTAN

MONGOLIA

NORTH KOREA

TAJIKISTAN

PAKISTAN

CHINA

(disputed border)

Beijing

Yellow River

Yellow Sea

Tibetan Plateau

Himalayas

NEPAL

Mount Everest

BHUTAN

(disputed border)

Yangtze River

Shanghai

East China Sea

INDIA

TAIWAN

MYANMAR

VIETNAM

Macao • Hong Kong

LAOS

South China Sea

7

CHAPTER 2

HISTORY

People have lived in China for thousands and thousands of years. Early groups often lived near the Yellow or Yangtze Rivers. They fished and farmed. Over time, small villages grew into cities.

The Shang were the first group to write down their history. They ruled northern China from roughly 1600 to 1046 BCE.

Studying objects made from stone and bronze helps people learn about China's ancient past.

The Silk Road was a network of many trade routes that stretched from China to Europe.

Then the Zhou **dynasty** took over. After that, leaders mainly ruled groups of small states. Wars sometimes broke out between them.

In 221 BCE, the Qin state united all of China. Its leader became China's first emperor. He led many building projects, including work on the Great Wall of China. The Han dynasty ruled next. Then small kingdoms broke off again. But later dynasties ruled all of China. The Tang and Ming were two examples. Both had large, powerful empires.

China's last dynasty was the Qing. It began in 1644 CE. During this dynasty, China grew even larger and stronger. But by the late 1800s, it was losing power.

TRADE TROUBLES

China has a long history of trade. The Silk Road brought goods to and from many countries. But some Europeans wanted more control. Britain fought two wars against China in the mid-1800s. Both times, China lost. More ports opened to foreign merchants. After the first war, Hong Kong became a British colony. It stayed under British control until 1997.

A **revolution** took place from 1911 to 1912. China became a republic. Its first president was Sun Yat-sen. But the new government didn't last long. Different political groups struggled for power. They included Nationalists and Communists. Communists wanted all property to be owned by the government. Nationalists opposed them. The two groups fought a civil war from 1945 to 1949.

The Communists won. They formed a new government. It was the People's Republic of China (PRC). Its first leader was Mao Zedong. He wanted to expand China's power. So, he started several programs. Some tried to make farms and

The Forbidden City is a huge palace in Beijing. Many Chinese emperors lived there.

factories produce more. Several of the changes caused major problems. But Mao enforced them anyway. He also tried to limit disagreement. People who opposed his ideas were often jailed or killed.

Mao died in 1976. After him, leaders made some major changes. They increased trade with other countries. China's **economy** grew very strong.

CHAPTER 3

CLIMATE, PLANTS, AND ANIMALS

Because China is so big, its climate varies widely. Western China doesn't get much rain. Yet **monsoons** bring rain to eastern China. The south gets heavy summer rains. Temperatures there can be quite hot. But the north has cold, snowy winters. Higher-up areas tend to be cooler as well.

Yaks live throughout the Tibetan Plateau and the Himalayas.

Zhangjiajie National Forest Park is in central China. The park is known for its tall, thin pillars of rock.

Deserts cover more than one-fourth of China. Most of these dry areas are in the north. The Gobi Desert is one. It is the biggest desert in Asia. Bare rock and sand stretch for miles. Some plants and animals, such as Bactrian camels, have adapted to survive the dryness.

Forests cover nearly one-fourth of China. The type varies by region. In the north, fir, pine, and spruce trees grow in boreal forests. Moose, minks, and many other animals live among them. Meanwhile, the south's rainforests are warm and wet. They provide homes for ferns, orchids, and tropical birds.

China's rivers also have many unique animals. Chinese alligators and Chinese giant salamanders are two examples.

GIANT PANDAS

China is the only country with wild giant pandas. These animals live in bamboo forests in western China. They spend 10 to 16 hours each day eating. Bamboo is their main food. So, people work to protect the forests. That way, the pandas have enough to eat.

CLIMATE CRISIS IN CHINA

BIG ISSUES

China uses a massive amount of energy each year. Coal and oil help power the country's cities, factories, and vehicles. As a result, China is the world's biggest producer of greenhouse gases. These gases contribute to **climate change**.

Climate change is already affecting China in many ways. One is heat. Recent years have had higher temperatures. Too much heat can make people and animals sick. They may even die. Warmer weather also melts snow and ice on mountains. For example, glaciers in the Himalayas are shrinking.

Warmer weather can cause problems for farmers. Crops may need more water. Or they may not grow as well. If that happens, people may run low on food.

Flooding is another big risk. Melting ice makes sea levels rise. And many of China's big cities

In 2020, more than 20 large floods hit cities throughout China.

are along the coast. Climate change can lead to stronger storms. It can also change their timing. For example, **typhoons** are happening earlier in the year. If this continues, they may hit during rainy season. Cities could be buried in water.

CHAPTER 4
RESOURCES, ECONOMY, AND GOVERNMENT

China has many natural resources. It is the world's top producer of both coal and waterpower. China also has sources of oil and natural gas. These fuels power many industries. In fact, China has one of the biggest economies in the world.

Manufacturing is a big industry in China. Mines throughout China produce

China produces about half of the world's coal. It also consumes about half of the coal used worldwide.

iron. Some iron is made into steel. Factories use these metals to make a wide variety of products, including machine parts and vehicles. Other factories produce plastics or fabrics. These materials are then used to make toys, clothing, and more. China also creates computers and other electronics. Its products are sold around the world.

More than one-fourth of people in China work in agriculture. Rice, wheat, and corn are the country's main crops. Farms also grow sugarcane, fruits, and vegetables. Many crops are shipped around the world. These include tea and spices.

China builds and sells more cars each year than any other country.

Service is another big industry. Many Chinese people work in health care or construction. Others have jobs related to tourism or education.

China has a strong central government. The Chinese Communist Party (CCP) runs it. The CCP makes rules about many areas of life, including **media** and education.

23

The National People's Congress makes China's laws. Its members are elected. But their roles are mainly ceremonial. They have little actual power. Instead, the CCP makes most decisions. It also influences China's courts and judges.

UYGHURS

About 12 million Uyghur people live in China. Most live in Northwest China. The Uyghurs are mostly Muslim. Many report being **persecuted** by China's government. Hundreds of thousands of Uyghurs have been jailed or sent to work camps. Children have been taken from their families. They are sent to boarding schools, which aim to erase their religion and culture. People around the world protest these actions. But China's government denies doing them.

Ürümqi is the capital of Xinjiang, an area in Northwest China with a somewhat separate government.

As a result, people who criticize or oppose the CCP may face danger.

A few areas, such as Hong Kong and Macao, have separate local governments. They've had more freedom to make their own laws. But in recent years, China's central government has tightened control.

CHAPTER 5

PEOPLE AND CULTURE

China is home to more than 1.4 billion people. More than 90 percent are Han Chinese. But the country has more than 50 other ethnic groups.

Mandarin is China's official language. However, people use several others. Some are linked to certain areas. For example, Cantonese is common in Guangdong.

> Guangzhou is one of China's five biggest cities. It's located in Guangdong province, an area near the southeast coast.

27

China is officially an atheist country. Yet millions of people practice religions. Faiths include Buddhism, Taoism, Islam, and Christianity. Several of these faiths have ties to China's history. For example, Taoism began in ancient China. So did Confucianism. Both explore the connection between mind, body, and spirit. As a result, their ideas sometimes blend together. They also helped inspire

CONFUCIUS

Confucius lived from 551 to 479 BCE. He was a well-known thinker who got his start working in government. He wanted to help people live peacefully. So, he taught ideas such as being honest and treating others with respect. People still study his teachings today.

Chinese painters often combine poems with scenes from nature.

martial arts, such as tai chi, which people around the world study and practice.

China has shaped many art forms. Its people have made beautiful pottery for thousands of years. Porcelain is one type. From China, it spread and sold around the world. Chinese painting and **calligraphy** also have long, influential traditions.

FOCUS QUESTIONS

Write your answers on a separate piece of paper.

1. Write a paragraph describing some of the main industries that China's economy relies on.

2. If you visited China, which plant or animal would you be most interested to see? Why?

3. What is the largest city in China?
- **A.** Shanghai
- **B.** Hong Kong
- **C.** Beijing

4. Why did China's ancient people live near rivers?
- **A.** for easy sources of water
- **B.** for large sources of steam power
- **C.** to avoid sources of germs

Answer key on page 32.

GLOSSARY

calligraphy
The art of beautiful writing.

climate change
A human-caused global crisis involving long-term changes in Earth's temperature and weather patterns.

dynasty
A series of rulers who all come from the same family.

economy
A system of goods, services, money, and jobs.

media
Ways of sharing information, such as books or videos, and the groups that create them.

monsoons
Strong winds that cause extreme wet and dry seasons in an area.

persecuted
Treated people cruelly or unfairly because of their beliefs or identity.

revolution
A complete change in a country's government, often a change that is sudden or violent.

typhoons
Strong storms with spinning winds that form over oceans.

TO LEARN MORE

BOOKS

Bell, Samantha S. *Ancient China*. Mendota Heights, MN: Focus Readers, 2020.

Kerry, Isaac. *Spotlight on China*. Minneapolis: Lerner Publications, 2024.

Lawrence, Blythe. *Great Wall of China*. Mendota Heights, MN: Focus Readers, 2023.

NOTE TO EDUCATORS

Visit **www.focusreaders.com** to find lesson plans, activities, links, and other resources related to this title.

INDEX

animals, 16–17, 18
art, 29

Beijing, 6–7

climate change, 18–19
Communist Party, 12, 23–25

dynasties, 10–11

economy, 13, 21

factories, 13, 18, 22
farming, 6, 9, 12, 18, 22

government, 12, 23–25, 28

Himalayas, 6–7, 18
Hong Kong, 7, 11, 25

languages, 27

Macao, 7, 25

Mao Zedong, 12–13

Nationalists, 12
natural resources, 21

religions, 24, 28

trade, 11, 13

Uyghurs, 24

Yangtze River, 6–7, 9
Yellow River, 6–7, 9

Answer Key: 1. Answers will vary; 2. Answers will vary; 3. A; 4. A